Dear Darling Gillian,

I can tell that you are a FORCE — please keep inspiring + leading the other ladies to achieve BALANCE like you!

Loads of Love

Abigail Carl
03/15/18

I  MY DOUBLES PARTNER!!!

AN INSPIRATIONAL TENNIS BOOK!!!

ADELINE ARJAD COOK

L♥VE
ALL
MEDIA

I 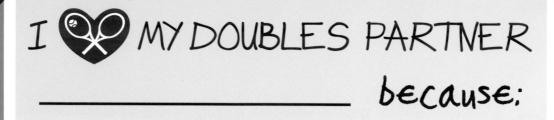 MY DOUBLES PARTNER

_____ because:

Insert Your
Tennis Partner's
Photo Here

L♥VE
ALL
MEDIA

Library of Congress Control Number: 2015919031

ISBN 978-0-9965958-2-7

Proudly printed in the United States of America on fine paper.

First printing hard cover December 2015.

I ♥ MY DOUBLES PARTNER!!!

I DEDICATE THIS BOOK TO:

MY PATIENT, KIND AND UNCONDITIONALLY LOVING HUSBAND ROBERT COOK.

AND FOR HIS FATHER WHO SERVED IN THE ARMY (THANK YOU) AND TAUGHT HIM TENNIS.

AND TO MY GRANDMA MAHIN ARJAD THE BIGGEST TENNIS LOVER.

AND TO ALL OF MY LOVELY DOUBLES PARTNERS.

AND MY FAIR OPPONENTS.

AND TO MY AWESOME CAPTAINS.

AND MY WONDERFUL COACHES.

AND MY PROFESSIONAL AND SWEET BOOK COACH JANICA SMITH.

AND MY INCREDIBLY TALENTED ILLUSTRATOR MELISSA CONTRERAS.

AND FINALLY TO THE UNITED STATES TENNIS ASSOCIATION (USTA).

I  YOU ALL!!!

TABLE OF CONTENTS

🎾🎾🎾🎾🎾

TABLE OF CONTENTS (CONT.)

A NOTE FROM ADELINE.....

I have written this book as a playful and fun reminder that tennis is our hobby – so let's make sure to have a great time and be nice!!!

I have used the court as my therapy through some tough times and have had many personal growth moments as a result of tough matches where I was physically hurt or mentally challenged. This game has magically transformed my relationship with myself – by self analysis and correction.

It also transformed the way I interacted with people – I realized that my energy on the court was powerful in my partner's and opponent's lives too!!! I became more responsible with my thoughts, actions and reactions.

Oh – and I lost 50 lbs too!!!

Loads of ♥ to you,
Adeline

I ❤️ MY DOUBLES PARTNER BECAUSE OF.....

GREAT FOOTWORK	NO EXCUSES
POSITIVE ATTITUDE	TOTAL MATCH FOCUS
1ST SERVES IN	GRACEFUL APPROACH SHOTS
HIGH TENNIS IQ	PERFECT FITNESS
INTEGRITY ON THE COURT	KINDNESS AND COMPASSION
CONSISTENCY	GREAT SPORTSMANSHIP
STRONG NET GAME	SHAKES OFF MISTAKES
AMAZING LOBS	SENSE OF HUMOR
INCREDIBLE BACKHANDS	TRICKY DROP SHOTS
MARVELOUS TOPSPIN	GREAT POINT CONSTRUCTION
POWERFUL OVERHEADS	FINDING THE OPEN SPACE
SNEAKY SLICES	NICE LOW SHOTS
AWESOME COURT SENSE	POSITIVITY
QUICK SELF CORRECTING	**AND MANY MORE ATTRIBUTES.....**

I picked up a tennis racquet for the first time in 2009. I was 36 years old and had become significantly overweight and I figured that tennis might be a fun way to get some much needed exercise. What I didn't figure on was falling head-over-heals in ♥ with the game.

It didn't take long before I was hooked. Unfortunately, tennis didn't seem to ♥ me back. I just couldn't keep the ball in the court. Instead of a source of exercise, tennis for me was an exercise in futility. Many tears of frustration were shed while soaking in my bathtub following day after day of struggling on the court. I might have continued that way indefinitely, but a severe case of tennis elbow sidelined me for several months. During that time away from the game, I had a chance to reflect and consider how I wanted to proceed. It was pretty apparent that I wasn't going to get any better just playing without instruction - so once my elbow healed up I started taking lessons. After a few lessons I improved enough to join a team. It was USTA 3.0 but I was on my way. Playing nearly every day over the following years I advanced to 3.5 and then to 4.0. I have so many amazing memories from playing in USTA league matches with my teams.

Tennis has also given me the opportunity to meet so many wonderful people. Between my coaches, teammates, doubles partners and opponents, I have developed friendships that I will cherish for the rest of my life. The tennis court is also where I happened to meet the ♥ of my life, Robert.

This book is to honor the instructors (and it took a village) who inspired me and all of the doubles partners with whom I have had the honor of playing.

Being a recreational tennis player, having fun on the court is my highest priority. Winning is nice too, but having a good time is really what it's all about for me. When playing doubles, my attitude about my partner has an influence on how much fun I have. It really helps if........

I ♥ MY DOUBLES PARTNER!!!

All doubles partners have positive and negative attributes. Some might have super cheerful dispositions but can't put away an overhead! Others can have incredible strokes but their attitude on the court suggests they don't even want to be there. So every time I step on the court I have to make a choice. If I choose to focus on the negative about my doubles partner, my attitude becomes negative and I don't have much fun on the court that day (and we usually lose the match too). So I choose to ♥ my doubles partner... no matter what. Doing that means be present to the positive!!!

Everyone has something to ♥ about them. And most of the time I have a pretty easy time "finding the ♥". Other times... not so much. In fact there have been days when I have thoroughly failed to ♥ my doubles partner, when I allowed negative perceptions to dominate my thoughts, leading to less-than-enjoyable tennis.

But I'm working on it! I always re-commit to ♥ !!!

One of the ways I decided to work on always loving my doubles partner was to think back to all the partners I had loved playing with over the years - and to write down something that I loved about each of them. I thought that remembering what I love about those doubles partners could help remind me to ♥ every doubles partner!!! So I started writing... and writing... and writing. It turns out that I've had quite a few lovable doubles partners in my relatively short tennis life. And those writings became the basis for this book.

Writing down what I ♥ about my doubles partner also helped me identify things we all can work on to make ourselves more lovable doubles partners. So I decided to include some of those thoughts in the book as well.

I hope that you enjoy reading....... *I* *MY DOUBLES PARTNER!!!*

♥
Adeline

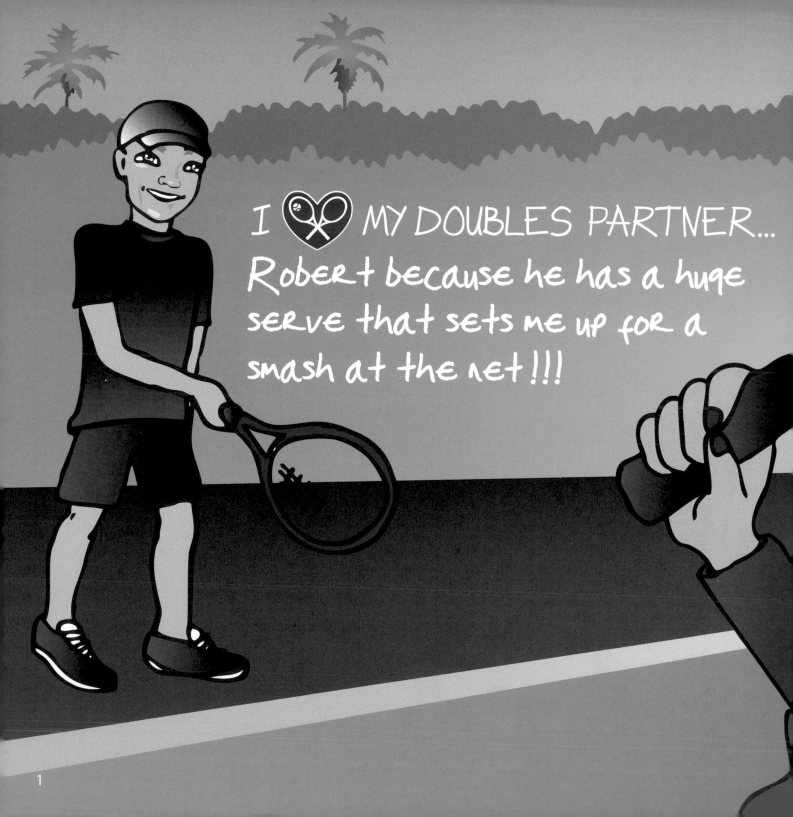

BE A
DOUBLES PARTNER
to
L♥VE

I ♥ MY DOUBLES PARTNER !!!
Not just like. Not just put up with.
LOVE them. There is always
something beautiful about their
game and their being.

"WHAT YOU FOCUS ON EXPANDS."

T HARV EKER

I ♡ MY DOUBLES PARTNER...
Mona because she stuns the
opponents with her beauty!!!

I 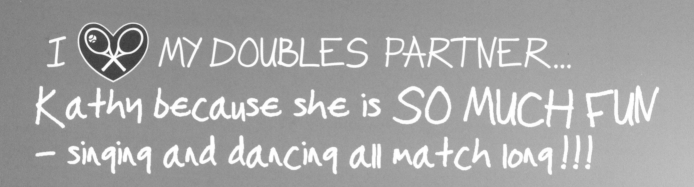 MY DOUBLES PARTNER...
Kathy because she is SO MUCH FUN
— singing and dancing all match long!!!

8

BE A
DOUBLES PARTNER
to
L♥VE

Be Fun. Remember that tennis is your hobby and if you want to have a good time then you have to BE a good time.

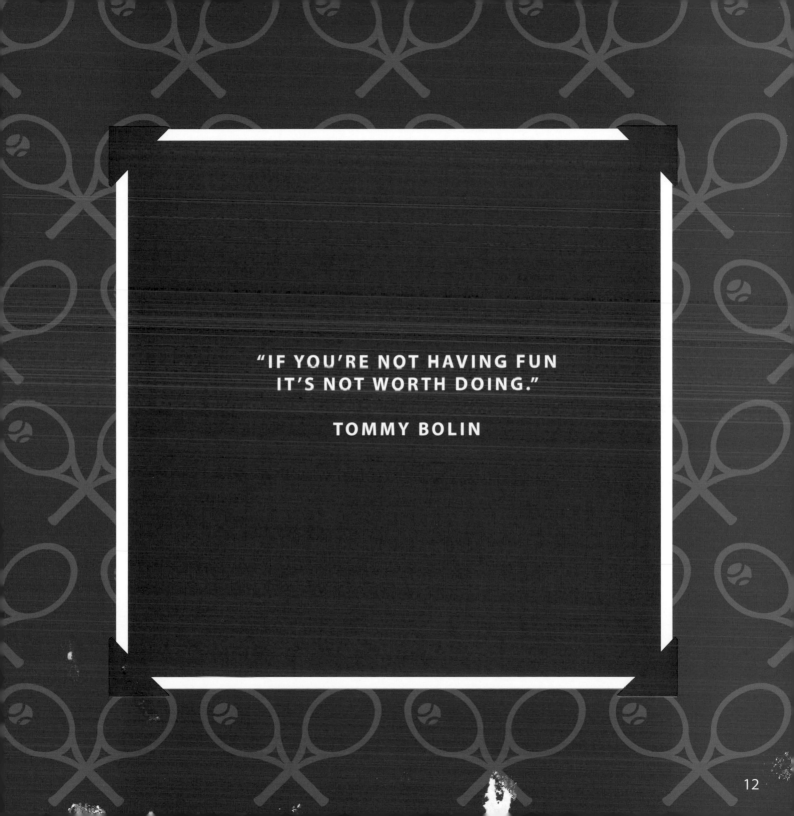

"IF YOU'RE NOT HAVING FUN
IT'S NOT WORTH DOING."

TOMMY BOLIN

I ♥ MY DOUBLES PARTNER...
Michelle because she has a
massive overhead that doesn't
just win the point, it scares the
opponents too !!!

I  MY DOUBLES PARTNER... Lisa because she always arrives early, warms up and is well prepared to play!!!

BE A
DOUBLES PARTNER
to
L♥VE

Be Committed. If you are going to compete then do so fully with passion and desire. Give 100% on the court every time.

"DO OR DO NOT – THERE IS NO TRY."

YODA

I 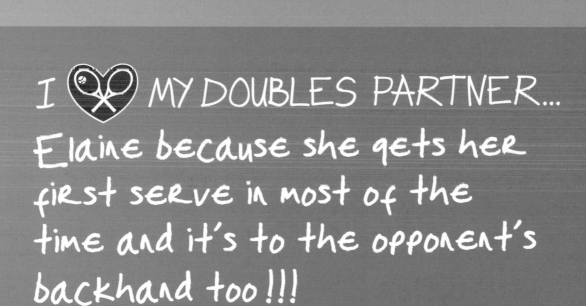 MY DOUBLES PARTNER...
Elaine because she gets her first serve in most of the time and it's to the opponent's backhand too!!!

I  MY DOUBLES PARTNER...
Leslie because she serves and
comes to the net to join me!!!

BE A
DOUBLES PARTNER
to
L♥VE

Allow for Magic.
When playing tennis stay in the
wonderment of the game. Take
deep pleasure in the unknown and
enjoy the surprises.

"LEARN TO LET THE MYSTERY, BE THE MYSTERY AND ACCEPT ITS MAGICAL GIFTS INTO YOUR LIFE."

BENTINHO MASSARO

I 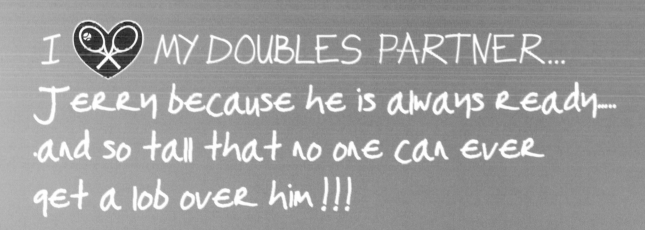 MY DOUBLES PARTNER...
Jerry because he is always ready....
.and so tall that no one can ever
get a lob over him!!!

I  MY DOUBLES PARTNER...
Michelle because she has the
most exciting backhand overhead
in tennis !!!

BE A
DOUBLES PARTNER
to
L♥VE

Be Tenacious. Stay in the point all the way until it ends. Run for balls even though they seem out of reach. Be in it to win it.

"ENDURANCE IS ONE OF THE MOST DIFFICULT DISCIPLINES, BUT IT IS TO THE ONE WHO ENDURES THAT THE FINAL VICTORY COMES."

BUDDHA

I ❤ MY DOUBLES PARTNER...
Amanda because she is flexible
and versatile — she plays either
side — deuce or ad!!!

I 🎾❤️ MY DOUBLES PARTNER... Heidi because she stays completely focused and committed on the court for the entire match!!!

BE A
DOUBLES PARTNER
to
L♥VE

Be Present. Keeping your mind on the court is very important. Do what you can to keep your focus on the ball and the match at all times.

"REALIZE DEEPLY THAT THE PRESENT MOMENT IS ALL YOU EVER HAVE."

ECKHART TOLLE

I ❤ MY DOUBLES PARTNER...
Albert because he hits a slice backhand that barely bounces up making it impossible to hit back !!!

I <3 MY DOUBLES PARTNER...
Lauren because she is willing to
implement any strategy that
I request!!!

BE A
DOUBLES PARTNER
to
L♥VE

Be Flexible. Taking into account your partner's viewpoint as well as your own — and trying their strategy too is always a great thing to do.

"STAY COMMITTED TO YOUR DECISIONS BUT STAY FLEXIBLE IN YOUR APPROACH."

TONY ROBBINS

I  MY DOUBLES PARTNER...
Jenny because she hits a relentless slice that makes the opponents crazy!!!

44

Sorry about that –
I need to step
into my shot

I <3 MY DOUBLES PARTNER...
Elisa because when she makes a
mistake she identifies the cause
and makes a quick correction !!!

BE A
DOUBLES PARTNER
to
L♥VE

Forgive Quickly.
When something happens that
upsets you – let it go – fast – and
find the learning or gift in it.

"TO TRANSFORM ENERGIES, WE MUST EXPERIENCE THEM TOTALLY, WORKING THROUGH THEM AND FORGIVING THEM, WHICH MEANS SEEING THE PERFECTION IN THEM."

COLIN TIPPING

I  MY DOUBLES PARTNER...
David because he is an optimist –
always expecting us to win and staying
positive throughout
the match!!!

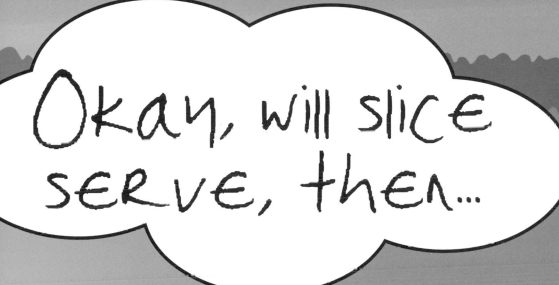

Okay, will slice serve, then...

I MY DOUBLES PARTNER...
Dede because she is the best
strategist I have ever met!!!
Her tennis IQ is at a genius level!!!

BE A
DOUBLES PARTNER
to
L♡VE

Pay Attention. Watch – learn – discuss and shift your game with your partner so that you have a plan to execute together.

"PLAN YOUR WORK AND
WORK YOUR PLAN."

LANDMARK EDUCATION

I 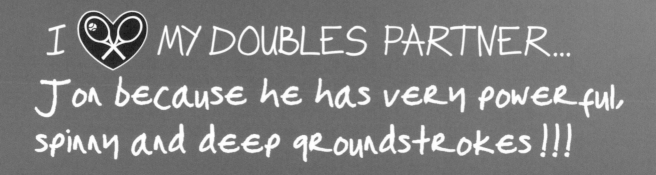 MY DOUBLES PARTNER...
Jon because he has very powerful, spinny and deep groundstrokes!!!

BE A
DOUBLES PARTNER
to
L♥VE

Play On High Ground. During and
after your matches be positive,
kind and respectful about your
partner and opponents.

"LET'S REMEMBER WHO WE REALLY ARE, WHICH IS SOULS, NOT EGOS."

RAM DASS

I  MY DOUBLES PARTNER...
Dawn because she always smells
so fresh and so clean!!!

VOWS! I promise to:

- Be sweet to you even if we are losing!
- Not gossip about you behind your back!
- Not tell you how to play tennis!
- Not blame YOU if I miss a shot!
- Not chastise you when you miss a shot!
- Not complain about the weather, wind, courts, my knee, my elbow......
- Be on YOUR team not the opponents!
- Avoid whining!
- Do my best to avoid you being SMASHED!
- Not micro manage your strategies!
- Not be negative about your serves, volleys, lobs, groundstrokes or overheads!
- Be right there with you on the court and not thinking about what I am making for dinner later!
- Do my best NOT to double fault (especially on game point)!
- Not talk consistently through the entire match!
- Attempt to PUT AWAY all overheads that you set me up for!
- Listen to your ideas of how to win!
- Fight for every point until the end!
- Play smart (instead of just trying to LOOK GOOD)!
- Take lessons and practice to GET BETTER!
- Be early for matches!
- Not teach you to play tennis ON or OFF the court!
- QUICKLY let go of tiffs that we may have on the court in a tense moment!

I will ♥ you through the fun easy matches, and the tough matches! Whether we win or lose, I will still RESPECT you and we will go to the next match CLOSER and STRONGER!!!

PRENUP: You will agree to know that I am doing the BEST that I can and if I make an error in a line call you have the authority to correct me, if I misspeak during the match you will forgive me and if I am not playing well you will know that I am doing the very best that I can – after all – I WANT TO WIN JUST AS MUCH AS YOU DO! That you will help us figure out what to change if we are losing! That, in the event of a divorce, it will be amicable and sweet!

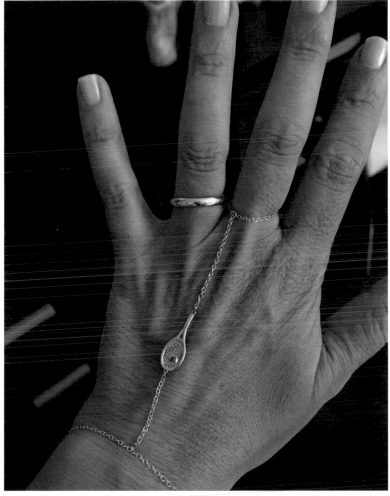

I have designed these beautiful gold and diamond hand jewels that I wear at all times (yes – even when playing tennis!!!). I use this as a reminder to be present, grateful and loving on the court at all times. They are available in yellow, white or rose gold at www.BLiSSbyAdeline.com

And they are handmade in Downtown Los Angeles.

I  MY DOUBLES PARTNER...
Christine because she stays completely calm, neutral and cool no matter what is going on !!!

BE A
DOUBLES PARTNER
to
L❤VE

Have Equanimity. Whatever
is happening on the court –
especially tense situations –
stay calm and grounded.

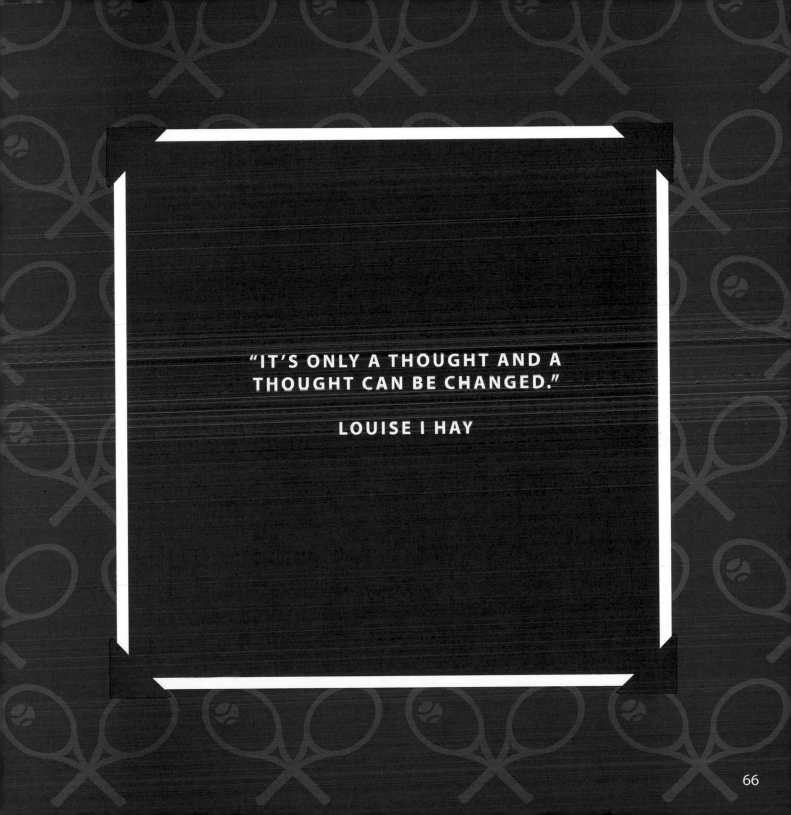

"IT'S ONLY A THOUGHT AND A THOUGHT CAN BE CHANGED."

LOUISE I HAY

I 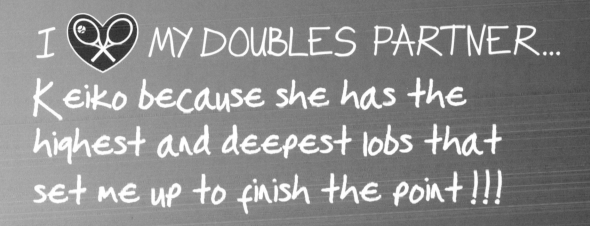 MY DOUBLES PARTNER...
Keiko because she has the highest and deepest lobs that set me up to finish the point !!!

I 🎾❤️ MY DOUBLES PARTNER... Melissa because she never gives up – she fights until the end no matter the score!!!

BE A
DOUBLES PARTNER
to
L♥VE

Be Supportive. Ask what
your partner needs to feel
connected with you. The two of
you must play as one.

"STRENGTH DOES NOT COME FROM WINNING, YOUR STRUGGLES DEVELOP YOUR STRENGTH."

MAHATMA GANDHI

I 🎾❤️ MY DOUBLES PARTNER...
Rachel because she hits the
hardest deepest backhand
groundstroke!!!

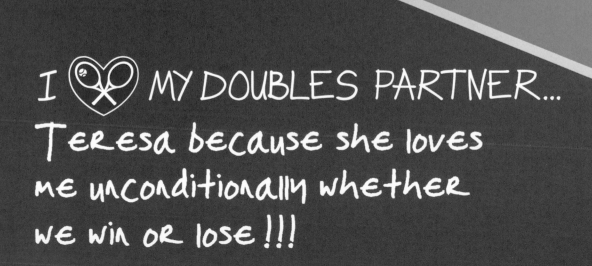

I <3 MY DOUBLES PARTNER...
Teresa because she loves
me unconditionally whether
we win or lose!!!

BE A
DOUBLES PARTNER
to
L♥VE

Be Generous. If your partner is making a lot of errors, stay sweet and lift them up. This is the only way to help them out of the rut.

"BE KIND, FOR EVERYONE YOU MEET
IS FIGHTING A HARD BATTLE."

PLATO

I 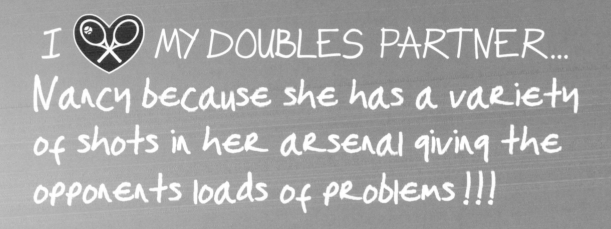 MY DOUBLES PARTNER...
Nancy because she has a variety
of shots in her arsenal giving the
opponents loads of problems!!!

I ♥ MY DOUBLES PARTNER...
Lorri because she has the kindest and biggest heart with loads of compassion and love!!!

BE A DOUBLES PARTNER to L🎾VE

Be kind. Remember that your partner is doing the best that they can in this moment so have compassion for them.

"KIND WORDS ARE SHORT AND EASY TO SPEAK BUT THEIR ECHOES ARE TRULY ENDLESS."

MOTHER TERESA

I ♡ MY DOUBLES PARTNER...
Janet because she has
an amazing swinging volley!!!

I 🎾❤️ MY DOUBLES PARTNER...
Tess because she stays so fit and
healthy on and off the court!!!

BE A
DOUBLES PARTNER
to
L♥VE

Be Healthy. Know your body well
and fuel it with only the finest
nutrition so that it performs
for you on the court.

"TAKE CARE OF YOUR BODY. IT'S THE ONLY PLACE YOU HAVE TO LIVE IN."

JIM ROHN

I  MY DOUBLES PARTNER...
Haideh because she hits drop shot volleys that the opponents can't even touch !!!

BE A
DOUBLES PARTNER
to
L♥VE

Learn. Every match, every
partner and every practice
is an opportunity for self
awareness and growth.

"DON'T WAIT FOR A GURU.
YOUR LIFE IS YOUR GURU."

KRISHNA DAS

I 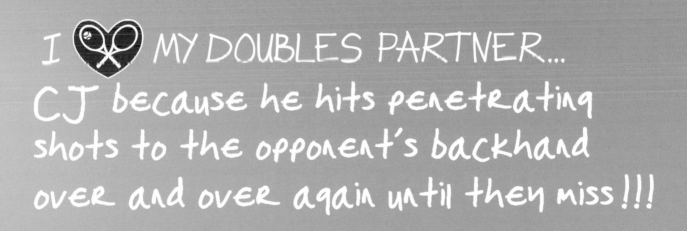 MY DOUBLES PARTNER...
CJ because he hits penetrating
shots to the opponent's backhand
over and over again until they miss !!!

I 🎾❤️ MY DOUBLES PARTNER...
Janine because she can smash an
overhead from the baseline !!!

BE A
DOUBLES PARTNER
to
L♥VE

Be Grateful. We are so lucky
to get to play tennis. We have
limbs, sight, agility, hand eye
coordination and breath.
Be thankful every day.

"HE IS A WISE MAN WHO DOES NOT GRIEVE FOR THE THINGS WHICH HE HAS NOT, BUT REJOICES FOR THOSE WHICH HE HAS."

EPICTETUS

I 🎾🎾 MY DOUBLES PARTNER... Yuriko because the woman doesn't miss!!! She is the most consistent player I have ever played with!!!

I MY DOUBLES PARTNER...
Bobby because he has a killer
inside out forehand!!!

BE A
DOUBLES PARTNER
to
L❤VE

LOVE ALL. Every match is a chance to open our hearts and let our divine light connect with the divine light of others.

"THE LOVE IS REAL IN ANY SITUATION EVERYTHING ELSE IS JUST AN ILLUSION."

MARIANNE WILLIAMSON

I 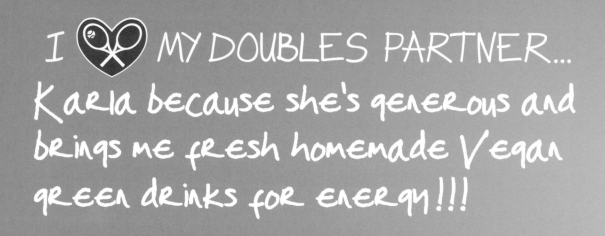 MY DOUBLES PARTNER...
Karla because she's generous and brings me fresh homemade Vegan green drinks for energy!!!

I ♡ MY DOUBLES PARTNER... Mary Anna because she is a generous tennis loving philanthropist !!!

BE A
DOUBLES PARTNER
to
L♥VE

Give Back. Whether you have a winning or losing season – write a sweet thank you note to your partner – and perhaps give them a gift too!

"A GENEROUS PERSON WILL PROSPER.
WHOEVER REFRESHES PEOPLE WILL
BE REFRESHED."

PROVERBS 11:25

I ♥ MY DOUBLES PARTNER...
Cindy because she is really enjoys
the game no matter what !!!

BE A
DOUBLES PARTNER
to
L♥VE

Be Playful. You can be fully present and committed yet light and happy at the same time – this is your hobby – enjoy every point.

"MOST SMILES ARE STARTED BY
ANOTHER SMILE."

FRANK A. CLARK

I 💚 MY DOUBLES PARTNER... Laura because she has the most incredible defensive volley that she turns into an offensive lob!!!

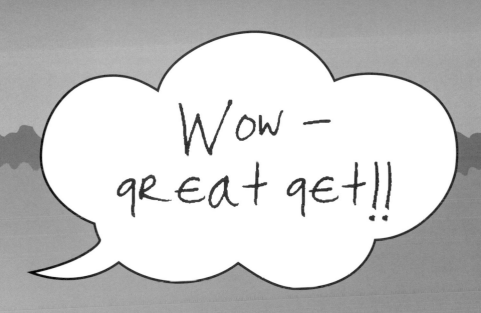

I 🎾❤️ MY DOUBLES PARTNER... Avryn because she has respect for my game and constantly compliments me!!!

BE A
DOUBLES PARTNER
to
L♥VE

Compliment Freely.
Notice and voice your partner's
positive attributes —
especially behind their back.

"EVERYBODY LIKES A COMPLIMENT."

ABRAHAM LINCOLN

I ♥ MY DOUBLES PARTNER...
Jerry because he mixes up the speed and location of his serves driving the opponents bonkers!!!

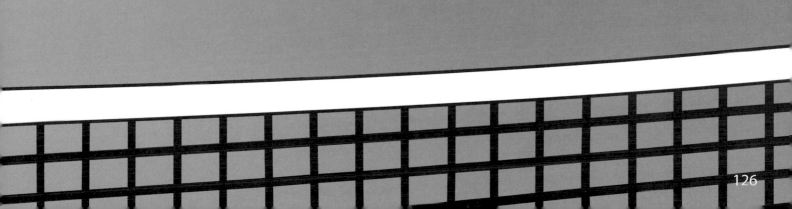

I 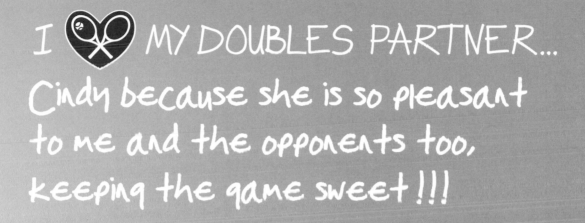 MY DOUBLES PARTNER...
Cindy because she is so pleasant
to me and the opponents too,
keeping the game sweet!!!

BE A
DOUBLES PARTNER
to
L♥VE

Be Gracious. Treat your partner, your opponents and the audience with good etiquette. Be courteous – they are our Sisters and Brothers.

"IT'S MORE IMPORTANT TO BE GRACIOUS THAN TO WIN."

DOROTHY KILGALLEN

I 💚 MY DOUBLES PARTNER...
Jessica because she disguises
her shots so well that the
opponents don't know where
she is going to hit !!!

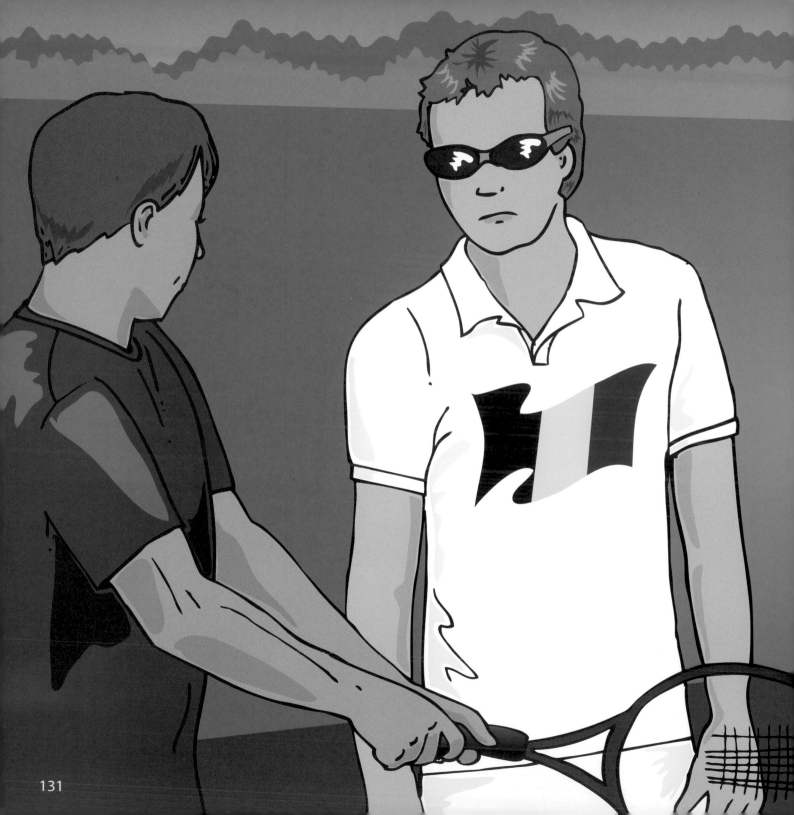

I ♥ MY DOUBLES PARTNER...
Jean-Marc because he is always taking lessons to improve his game!!!

BE A
DOUBLES PARTNER
to
L♥VE

Be Lucky. Walk on the court knowing that you have practiced enough and that all of the forces are on your side.

"LUCK IS WHAT HAPPENS WHEN PREPARATION MEETS OPPORTUNITY."

LUCIUS ANNAEUS SENECA

I ♡ MY DOUBLES PARTNER...
Michelle because she gets so low for her strokes and smacks them!!!

137

I ❤ MY DOUBLES PARTNER...
Kumi because she communicates so well on the court — I always know which balls are mine!!!

138

BE A
DOUBLES PARTNER
to
L♥VE

Elevate Your Partner. Make sure that you make your shot choices in accordance with your partner's strengths so they get to hit their best ball.

"MASTERING OTHERS IS STRENGTH.
MASTERING YOURSELF IS
TRUE POWER"

LAO TZU

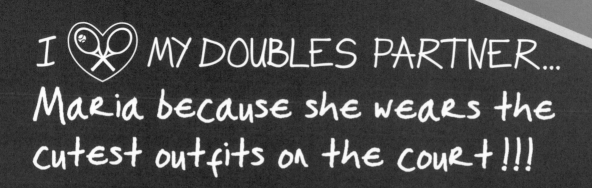

I 🎾❤️ MY DOUBLES PARTNER...
Maria because she wears the
cutest outfits on the court!!!

You are #1, Adeline –
the best!!!

I ♥ MY DOUBLES PARTNER...
Jay because he helps me
feel confident and powerful
on the court!!!

BE A
DOUBLES PARTNER
to
L🎾VE

Be Fearless. Walk onto the court knowing that there is nothing to lose at all. Stand up straight and trust your game.

"FAITH IS TAKING THE FIRST STEP
EVEN WHEN YOU DON'T SEE THE
WHOLE STAIRCASE."

MARTIN LUTHER KING JR

I  MY DOUBLES PARTNER... Dalton because his tremendous wing span makes it very difficult for the opponents to get the ball past him!!!

148

I ❤ MY DOUBLES PARTNER...
Mary because she has the most
angelic and kind energy of anyone
I have ever met !!!

BE A
DOUBLES PARTNER
to
L♥VE

Be In Flow. Accept and welcome all that is. Allow the sun, the wind, the shadows or the temperature to be a gift to you.

"THE PURPOSE OF OUR LIVES
IS TO BE HAPPY."

DALAI LAMA

153

I ❤ MY DOUBLES PARTNER...
Yolanda because she hits consistent heavy topspin groundstrokes until the opponents eventually miss!!!

I  MY DOUBLES PARTNER... Sergio because he plays classical tennis and has beautiful strokes !!!

156

BE A
DOUBLES PARTNER
to
L♥VE

Own It. You are 100% responsible for your thoughts, words and actions. You have great power, think and act wisely.

"THE GREATEST DISCOVERY OF ALL OF TIME IS THAT A PERSON CAN CHANGE HIS FUTURE BY MERELY CHANGING HIS ATTITUDE."

OPRAH WINFREY

I 🎾 MY DOUBLES PARTNER...
Kristin because she steps into her volleys making them tremendously powerful and hard to return!!!

I 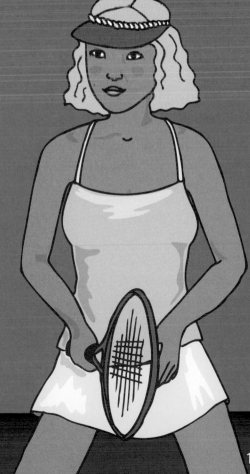 MY DOUBLES PARTNER...
Akiko because she will do any formation like "I" or "Australian" or even a weird one "Australian both back"!!!

162

BE A
DOUBLES PARTNER
to
L♥VE

Give Space. Your partner will make mistakes in matches – stay focused on their good intentions and not the results.

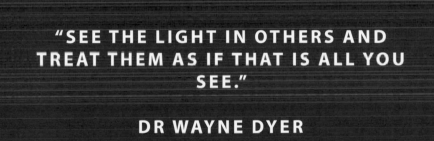

"SEE THE LIGHT IN OTHERS AND
TREAT THEM AS IF THAT IS ALL YOU
SEE."

DR WAYNE DYER

I ♥ MY DOUBLES PARTNER...
Dean because he can hit a volley from the baseline that can win the point !!!

I ♥ MY DOUBLES PARTNER...
Carrie because she has a huge down the line shot that passes the opponents with ease!!!

BE A
DOUBLES PARTNER
to
L♥VE

Go For It. Make sure that you play the way that you want to so that you leave it all on the court. When you go home, be proud.

"JUST GO OUT THERE AND DO WHAT
YOU HAVE TO DO."

MARTINA NAVRATILOVA

I  MY DOUBLES PARTNER...
Jennifer because she smacks
her volleys deep and behind the
opponents feet so they can't
even touch them!!!

I ♥ MY DOUBLES PARTNER... Teri because she hits so deep with topspin that it puts the opponents on the defensive !!!

174

BE A
DOUBLES PARTNER
to
L♡VE

Love Yourself. Be kind and complimentary to yourself. Focus on your strengths and acknowledge your great shots.

"YOU DON'T NEED TO BE ACCEPTED BY OTHERS. YOU NEED TO ACCEPT YOURSELF."

THICH NHAT HANH

I ❤ MY DOUBLES PARTNER...
Sal because he has the best
hands — the opponents can
never finish the point !!!

I 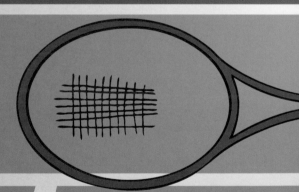 MY DOUBLES PARTNER...
Sylvanie because she has incredible anticipation — she knows where the opponents are going to hit !!!

BE A DOUBLES PARTNER to L♥VE

Self Confidence.
It is important to have strong body language when walking on the court. It will grow your partner's trust and opponent's fear.

"SELF CONFIDENCE IS THE FIRST
REQUISITE TO GREAT UNDERTAKINGS."

SAMUEL JOHNSON

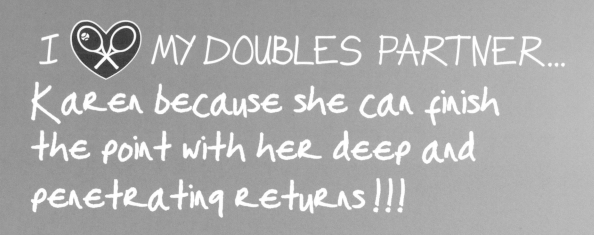

I ♥ MY DOUBLES PARTNER...
Karen because she can finish
the point with her deep and
penetrating returns !!!

184

I 🎾❤️ MY DOUBLES PARTNER...
Alia because she always has a
contagious broad smile on her face!!!

I 🎾 MY DOUBLES PARTNER... Christy because she has the best court ethics!!!

BE A
DOUBLES PARTNER
to
L♥VE

Be Happy. You are the director of your emotional state — no one on the court can make you react — stay blissful at any cost.

"USE ANY EXCUSE TO FEEL GOOD
AND SEE WHAT HAPPENS."

ABRAHAM-HICKS

I 💚 MY DOUBLES PARTNER... Adele because she is so fast she gets to every ball !!!

I 🎾 MY DOUBLES PARTNER...
Pam because she recognizes
when a strategy isn't working
and switches it up immediately!!!

BE A
DOUBLES PARTNER
to
L♥VE

Be Creative. Don't let your opponents get too comfortable — change your shots and strategies to keep them guessing what's next.

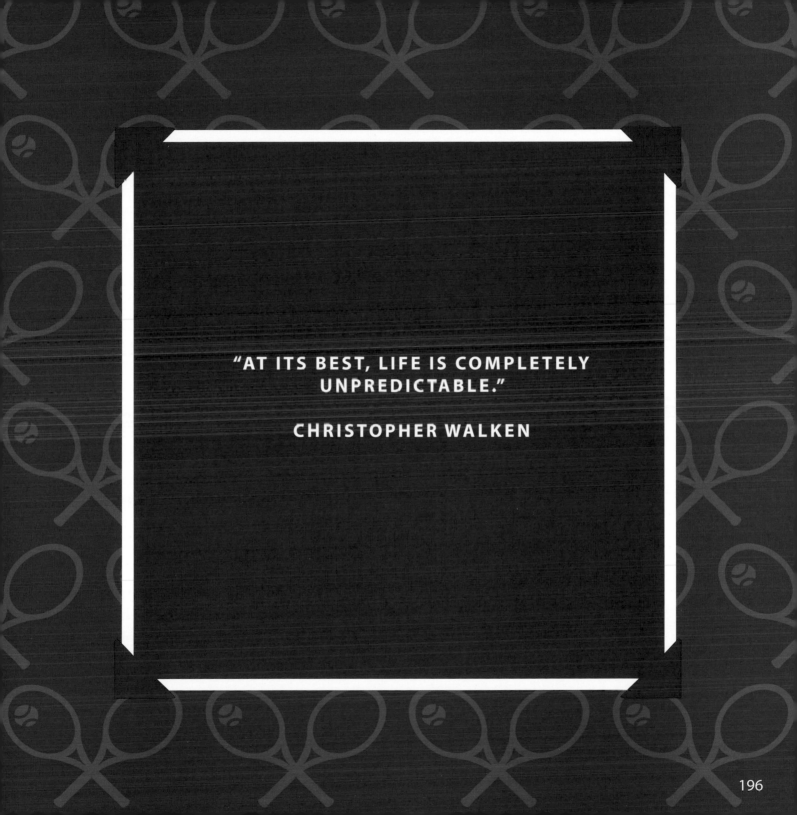

"AT ITS BEST, LIFE IS COMPLETELY UNPREDICTABLE."

CHRISTOPHER WALKEN

I 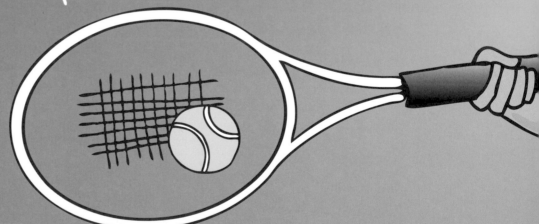 MY DOUBLES PARTNER...
Allison because she has the
hardest and flattest ground
strokes that land at the
opponent's feet !!!

Let's talk about it...

I 🎾❤️ MY DOUBLES PARTNER...
Rikki because she is most able to work through issues quickly and get back on track to winning!!!

BE A
DOUBLES PARTNER
to
L♥VE

Communicate. This is a team sport and having the same strategy is uber important for success.

"COMMUNICATION MUST BE HOT.
THAT'S HONEST, OPEN AND
TWO-WAY."

DAN OSWALD

I ❤ MY DOUBLES PARTNER...
Beverly because she can handle balls from the service line, making it hard to pass her !!!

I  MY DOUBLES PARTNER... Jacqueline because she moves around at the net and distracts the opponents!!!

I ♥ MY DOUBLES PARTNER...
Ande because she is light on
her feet so keeps engaged in
every point !!!

I  MY DOUBLES PARTNER...
Jason because he is so aggressive at the net that he takes most of the balls and finishes the point for me !!!

BE A
DOUBLES PARTNER
to
L♥VE

Be Coachable. Consider that your partner may have some valuable insight into your game and be open to their ideas. Be grateful for the help.

"YOU MUST ALWAYS BE THE APPRENTICE, EVEN WHEN YOU BECOME THE MASTER."

CHRISTOPHER CUMBY

I  MY DOUBLES PARTNER...
Lisa because she is highly
energetic throughout the
whole match!!!

I ♥ MY DOUBLES PARTNER...
Terry because she makes
the most honest line calls —
if it's close it's in !!!

BE A
DOUBLES PARTNER
to
L♥VE

Be Honest. Integrity is vital in the game of tennis. Keep your calls generous and win only knowing that you actually earned every point.

"SUCCESS WITHOUT
INTEGRITY IS FAILURE."

UNKNOWN

I ♥ MY DOUBLES PARTNER... Yuki because she knows exactly when the ball is good enough to close the net !!!

BE A
DOUBLES PARTNER
to
L♡VE

Be Positive. Optimism has a way
of creating confidence and wins.
The more you trust yourself
and your partner –
the better the outcome.

"IF YOU CAN DREAM IT -
YOU CAN ACHIEVE IT."

WILLIAM ARTHUR WARD

I 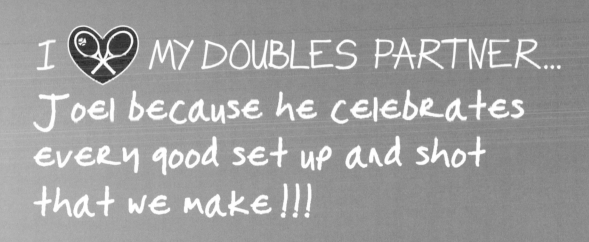 MY DOUBLES PARTNER... Joel because he celebrates every good set up and shot that we make!!!

BE A DOUBLES PARTNER to L♥VE

Let Go. As a recreational player being on the court is the win. Try your best but don't be so attached to the result that you lose sight of the fun.

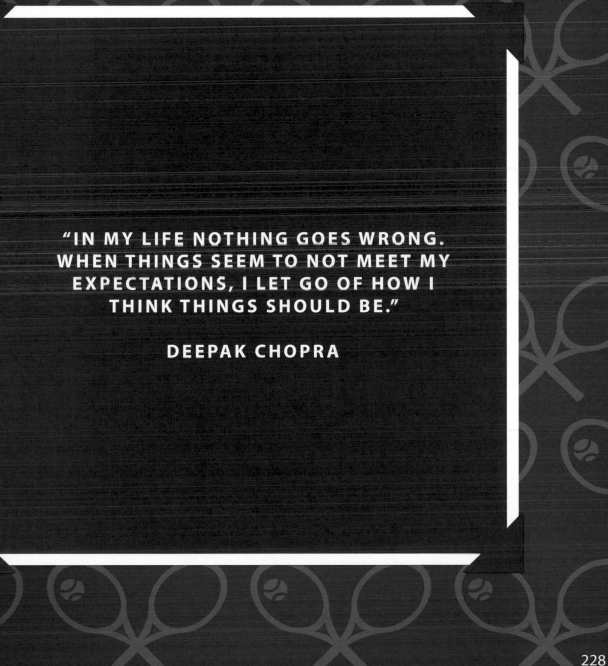

"IN MY LIFE NOTHING GOES WRONG. WHEN THINGS SEEM TO NOT MEET MY EXPECTATIONS, I LET GO OF HOW I THINK THINGS SHOULD BE."

DEEPAK CHOPRA

I 🎾❤️ MY DOUBLES PARTNER...
Jennifer because her ground
strokes are so hard and low
over the net that I get
overheads to smash!!!

I 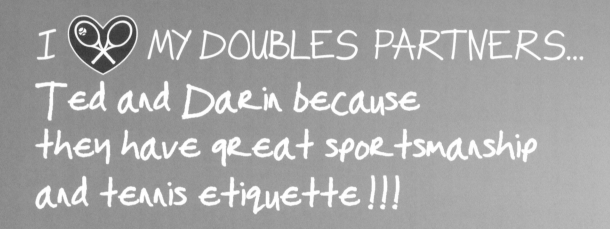 MY DOUBLES PARTNERS...
Ted and Darin because
they have great sportsmanship
and tennis etiquette!!!

I PLAY TENNIS TO HAVE FUN!!!

IT'S MY HOBBY. A TIME TO LAUGH AND BE SOCIAL.

When I first started playing, the fun was **automatic**. Even through the initial frustrations and struggles learning the game, tennis was new and exciting and just being on the court was fun. And I was so busy thinking about how to hit the ball and play the game that nothing could distract me from my overall happiness.

As my tennis game improved, the fun was no longer automatic. Once it didn't require every ounce of my concentration just to get the ball over the net, I started becoming more aware of other things on the court. So if other players had a negative attitude, or were unkind, or made "questionable" line calls, I noticed. And because I have a tendency to take others' behavior personally, I allowed those behaviors to impact my happiness.

Suddenly, something I did **specifically for fun** was not always fun. There were days when I would step off the court feeling decidedly less happy than I did before playing.

This was worrisome.

I had previously made a **commitment to happiness**. A serious commitment. I had even started a company based on the concept: **BLiSS** by Adeline. I had worked very hard to define, establish and maintain a state of BLiSS in every area of my life…except tennis.

It wasn't that I had neglected tennis in this regard, it's just that tennis never needed any help being **BLiSS**ful before.

Now it did.

And so I started looking at how I could apply to tennis what I had learned about BLiSS in other areas of my life.

First of all, I had to **accept responsibility** for my own happiness in tennis. Happiness is a choice. No one can "make" us happy, or unhappy for that matter. While it is possible for others to influence our happiness, enabling or discouraging it as the case may be, ultimately, it is our choice to be happy or not. So I needed to **choose BLiSS** for tennis.

So I did.

Once I decided to commit to happiness in tennis, the next step was to figure out how to get there and STAY there, regardless of the circumstances on the court.

There are so many things that can contribute to overall happiness that I felt a need to narrow it down to behaviors that had worked for me before and that would be easily applied on the tennis court. My conclusion was the following formula:

TENACITY + GENEROSITY + GRATITUDE = BLiSS

Here are some of the things that I am currently working on to ensure more fun for myself and others on the courts:

TENACITY:

Tennis is my hobby but it is also competitive. When I first started playing tennis, the point was to WIN! Now - **my focus is on enjoyment** - not winning   but of course improving and doing my best is very fun indeed. Pushing my limits and growing my tennis IQ has a deep satisfying pleasure in itself. The reason that tenacity is important for my fun is that I do need discipline in my behavior in order to stay healthy and happy on the courts. There have been times when I didn't hydrate the night before and got cramps in my match the next day, or my lack of lessons at the beginning had me holding the racquet wrong causing tennis elbow! It's important to **play consciously to be in good health** for your matches.

Some of the things I do to increase my performance and confidence on the court:

- Continue to take lessons to improve my technique
- Read great tennis books to increase my knowledge
- Eat nutritious foods for physical health
- Be coachable and open to learning
- Stretch after matches to prevent injury
- Stay hydrated to avoid cramping
- Keep my body fat low to reduce stress on my joints
- Commit to strength training to increase speed and power
- Play with people of all levels and styles
- Meditate daily to strengthen my focus and presence

GENEROSITY:

Being uptight and rigid with your partner on the court makes for a terrible match. We are all born of different parents, in different circumstances and with **radically different points of view** of how things "should" be. Trying to get everyone to behave how I deem appropriate will not make for a pleasurable experience. Being generous doesn't just pertain to your partner - also to your coaches, your opponents, people watching and **yourself too**! We are ALL doing the best that we can in this moment with the knowledge and energy that we have. We are all vibrating at different tones, and no one is "wrong" - they are just reacting with their own stuff. The best way to have BLiSS on the courts is to just allow everyone to be who they are and LOVE them for it. ESPECIALLY the horrible people - only hurt people hurt people - so they need the most love and kindness of us all. Send them love and light on their journey!

The interesting thing about being generous is that it really affects MY joy on the court. When I am going with the flow of the match, the weather, the opponents, the noise level, the court conditions and the attitude of my partner - I notice a distinct elevation of my own pleasure!!! And when I notice my mind wandering into the negative abyss of how things "should be" - I **gently return to my breath** and very kindly tell myself that "all is well for myself and others." It is very important **for my happiness** to give the ultimate generosity of allowing things to **be just as they are** without a need to direct and control them.

Here are some ways that I am generous in my matches:

- Giving a smile, even when I'm not at my happiest
- Giving compliments to good shots, effort made and well-played points
- Giving kindness, even when it doesn't feel "deserved" or reciprocated
- Giving my partner my best effort, even when I really don't feel like it
- Giving my partner my presence, seeking to meet his or her needs on the court
- Opening a can of balls before anyone else
- Having humility about my attributes
- Being very generous with my line calls

GRATITUDE:

When I first started playing tennis, I was just **so grateful** that I was on the court. Every ball in was a huge celebration! And when someone wanted to be my doubles partner, it was pure happiness. I was very **excitable, fun and playful** on the court. As I became more experienced, I also became more "bratty." My expectation of myself and others grew - and with that - so did my disappointments. I found myself sighing on the court. Rolling my eyes. Annoyed at the weather. Peeved about noises on the streets. Trying to control my opponents' behavior. Giving the evil eye look to the audience if they clapped at the "wrong" time. None of these things contributed to my love of the game. The more I focused on the things that I didn't like - the more I hated playing tennis. **I knew it was time for a change.** So I stopped complaining and became grateful.

Here are some of the things that I am currently grateful for:

- Having the physical ability to play
- Living in sunny Southern California
- Having the financial resources to afford tennis clothes, equipment and court fees
- Having good hand-eye coordination to hit the shots I want (most of the time)
- Being around other tennis lovers
- Having the time to do a hobby that I love

Tennis has been the **biggest teacher** for me. It has been my therapy. Day by day I am improving as a WOMAN from the lessons that I learn on the court. And for me - it all comes down to this one thing - learning to ♥ ALL. I hope that you join me in this mission of practicing compassion and ♥ on and off the court too!!!

Adeline

TENNIS BOOKS THAT I !!!

WINNING UGLY: MENTAL WARFARE IN TENNIS
BY BRAD GILBERT

OPEN: AN AUTOBIOGRAPHY
BY ANDRE AGASSI

NICK BOLLETTIERI'S TENNIS HANDBOOK
BY NICK BOLLETTIERI

THE INNER GAME OF TENNIS
BY W. TIMOTHY GALLWEY

THE ART OF DOUBLES: WINNING TENNIS STRATEGIES AND DRILLS
BY PAT BLASKOWER

FOCUSED FOR TENNIS: FEATURING THE 3-R'S MENTAL TRAINING SYSTEM
BY KARL A. SLAIKEU PH.D. AND ROBERT TROGOLO

WINNING IN TENNIS AND LIFE
BY MARY PAT FALEY

I  MY COACH!!!!

IF IT WASN'T FOR THESE WONDERFUL TENNIS TEACHERS - I WOULD NOT BE THE PLAYER I AM TODAY.

ROBERT TROGOLO, who was the man responsible for teaching me top spin!!!
https://en.wikipedia.org/wiki/Robert_Trogolo - Austin, Texas

ROSIE GARZA, who taught me to be present with the ball and on the court!!!
Director of Tennis, Courtyard Tennis and Swim Club - Austin, Texas

RON GUSE, who made me move my feet!!!
https://twitter.com/ronguse - Austin, Texas

BEVERLY BOWES-HACKNEY, who taught me to be confident!!!
http://tinyurl.com/beverlyboweshackney - Austin, Texas

KURT ROTHMAN, who taught me doubles strategy!!!
Ernie Howlett Park - Rolling Hills Estates, California

DAN JOHNSTON, who taught me to move in at the right time!!!
West End Racquet and Health Club – Torrance, California

SAL BARBARO, who taught me soft hands at the net!!!
Director of Tennis - Omni Amelia Island Plantation - Fernandina Beach, Florida

JASON WILKS, who taught me tenacity!!!
jasonb.wilks@gmail.com - Stuart, Florida

TREVOR SANDS, who taught me to step into my shots!!!
Griffin Club LA - Los Angeles, California

JOSEPH FURIOSO, who taught me to be healthy!!!
Pro Manager – Caswell Tennis Center – Austin, Texas

NICK BOLLETTIERI, who taught me early racquet preparation!!!
http://www.nickbollettieri.com - Bradenton, Florida

JEFF SALZENSTEIN, who taught me the importance of stretching!!!
www.jeffsalzensteintennis.com - Denver, Colorado

THINGS I 🎾❤️ IN TENNIS......

PEOPLE I 🎾❤ IN TENNIS......

IF YOU ♥ MY BOOK PLEASE CONNECT WITH ME!!!

f : WWW.FACEBOOK.COM/ILOVEMYDOUBLESPARTNER

📷 : WWW.INSTAGRAM.COM/ILOVEMYDOUBLESPARTNER

🐦 : @LOVEMYDOUBLES

E-MAIL: ILOVEMYDOUBLESPARTNER@GMAIL.COM

PHONE: 310.701.7171

IF YOU WOULD LIKE TO BUY MORE BOOKS…………..

OR CUTE *I ♥ MY DOUBLES PARTNER* WATER BOTTLES,
HATS, T-SHIRTS, TENNIS BAG TAGS OR

EVEN A BEAUTIFUL GOLD AND DIAMOND
HAND JEWEL OR NECKLACE………….

PLEASE VISIT MY WEBSITE AT:
WWW.ILOVEMYDOUBLESPARTNER.COM

AND MAKE IT A SWEET DAY
(AFTER ALL A DAY ON THE COURTS
IS ALWAYS BETTER THAN A DAY AT WORK!!!)

♥♥♥♥♥♥♥♥♥♥